EMMANUEL JOSEPH

The Legacy We Carry, Stories of Family, Community, and the Creative Spark That Endures

Copyright © 2025 by Emmanuel Joseph

All rights reserved. No part of this publication may be reproduced, stored or transmitted in any form or by any means, electronic, mechanical, photocopying, recording, scanning, or otherwise without written permission from the publisher. It is illegal to copy this book, post it to a website, or distribute it by any other means without permission.

First edition

This book was professionally typeset on Reedsy.
Find out more at reedsy.com

Contents

1	Chapter 1: Roots of Our Journey	1
2	Chapter 2: Threads of Tradition	3
3	Chapter 3: A Tapestry of Stories	5
4	Chapter 4: Echoes of the Past	7
5	Chapter 5: The Bonds That Bind	9
6	Chapter 6: Guardians of Wisdom	11
7	Chapter 7: Celebrations of Life	13
8	Chapter 8: Journeys of Discovery	15
9	Chapter 9: The Power of Resilience	17
10	Chapter 10: Threads of Connection	19
11	Chapter 11: The Spirit of Generosity	21
12	Chapter 12: The Journey of Change	23
13	Chapter 13: The Spirit of Innovation	25
14	Chapter 14: The Strength of Unity	27
15	Chapter 15: The Role of Mentorship	29
16	Chapter 16: The Journey of Healing	31
17	Chapter 17: A Legacy of Hope	33
18	Chapter 18: The Essence of Identity	35
19	Chapter 19: A Legacy of Love	37

1

Chapter 1: Roots of Our Journey

The heart of every family tree is its roots, nourishing and anchoring each branch. For centuries, our ancestors wove tales of resilience, love, and perseverance into the fabric of their daily lives. These stories were more than mere folklore; they were living testaments to their spirits and values. Each generation added new layers, creating a rich tapestry of tradition, belief, and wisdom. From the whispered bedtime stories to the grand narratives shared around bonfires, the legacy we inherit is steeped in the essence of those who came before us.

In the bustling market squares and quiet village huts, the convergence of diverse communities created a mosaic of culture and identity. The old cobblestone streets echoed with the laughter of children and the fervent discussions of elders. Here, in these communal spaces, the true essence of family extended beyond bloodlines. Bonds formed through shared experiences, collective struggles, and mutual support. The traditions and customs evolved, blending into a symphony of voices and perspectives, all contributing to the narrative of our shared heritage.

At the heart of this vibrant community lay the creative spark that fueled innovation and imagination. Artisans, storytellers, and musicians were the custodians of this creative spirit. Their craft was a reflection of their environment, a dialogue between the past and present. Through their works, they immortalized the beauty of everyday life and the profound moments of joy and sorrow. Their creativity was not just a form of expression; it was a bridge that connected generations, allowing the wisdom of the past to illuminate the future.

As we navigate the complexities of the modern world, we carry with us the legacy of our forebears. Their stories, sacrifices, and triumphs shape our identities and inform our choices. The values they instilled in us - resilience, compassion, and creativity - continue to guide us as we forge our paths. In honoring their legacy, we find the strength to overcome challenges and the inspiration to create our own stories. Our journey is not just a continuation of theirs; it is a testament to the enduring power of family, community, and the creative spark that binds us all.

2

Chapter 2: Threads of Tradition

Tradition is the thread that weaves through the fabric of our lives, creating a sense of continuity and belonging. Each ritual, festival, and custom holds a story that connects us to our past. From the vibrant dances of harvest celebrations to the solemn observances of ancestral worship, these traditions are a testament to the ingenuity and spirit of our forebears. They remind us of the values that have been cherished for generations and inspire us to uphold them in our own lives.

In every corner of the world, communities have developed unique traditions that reflect their environment, history, and values. The rhythmic drumming of a village festival, the intricate patterns of traditional attire, and the mouthwatering aromas of age-old recipes all tell a story. These traditions are not static relics; they evolve with time, adapting to the changing needs and circumstances of the community. Yet, their core essence remains unchanged, serving as a beacon of identity and pride.

The transmission of tradition is a sacred responsibility, often passed down through generations within families. Grandparents become the custodians of knowledge, sharing their wisdom and experiences with younger members. Through stories, songs, and hands-on practices, they instill a sense of respect and appreciation for the legacy that has been entrusted to them. This intergenerational bond is a cornerstone of community, fostering a deep sense of connection and continuity.

THE LEGACY WE CARRY, STORIES OF FAMILY, COMMUNITY, AND THE CREATIVE SPARK THAT ENDURES

As we navigate the complexities of modern life, the threads of tradition offer us a sense of grounding and purpose. They remind us of who we are and where we come from, providing a framework for our values and actions. In honoring these traditions, we pay homage to our ancestors and ensure that their legacy endures. The creative spark that ignited these traditions continues to burn brightly within us, guiding us as we forge new paths while staying true to our roots.

3

Chapter 3: A Tapestry of Stories

Every family has its own tapestry of stories, woven together through generations of shared experiences. These stories are the lifeblood of our heritage, capturing the triumphs, struggles, and moments of profound connection that define us. From the adventurous tales of ancestors who braved new frontiers to the intimate recollections of everyday life, these narratives shape our understanding of ourselves and the world around us.

In the quiet moments of reflection, we often find ourselves drawn to the stories of our past. These tales, passed down through oral tradition or recorded in dusty journals, offer us a glimpse into the lives of those who came before us. They reveal the choices and sacrifices that have paved the way for our present, and the values that have been cherished and upheld through generations. Each story is a thread in the intricate tapestry of our family's legacy, contributing to the rich mosaic of our identity.

The act of storytelling is a powerful tool for preserving and transmitting our heritage. It is through stories that we connect with our ancestors, bridging the gap between past and present. These narratives are not mere recollections; they are living entities that evolve with each retelling, adapting to the changing context and perspectives of the storyteller. In this way, the stories of our family become a dynamic and ever-evolving testament to our collective journey.

As we continue to weave new stories into the tapestry of our family's legacy, we honor the creativity and resilience of those who came before us. Their experiences and lessons serve as a guiding light, illuminating the path ahead. In sharing our own stories, we contribute to the ongoing narrative of our heritage, ensuring that the creative spark that has been passed down through generations continues to burn brightly. Our stories are a testament to the enduring power of family, community, and the creative spirit that binds us all.

4

Chapter 4: Echoes of the Past

The echoes of the past resonate within us, shaping our thoughts, actions, and aspirations. Each generation leaves an indelible mark on the tapestry of our heritage, contributing to the legacy we carry forward. The stories of our ancestors, their struggles, and triumphs, serve as a reminder of the resilience and strength that flows through our veins. These echoes, though faint, are a powerful testament to the enduring spirit of those who came before us.

In the quiet moments of introspection, we often find ourselves reflecting on the lives of our ancestors. Their experiences, though separated by time, offer valuable lessons and insights that guide us in our own journeys. The challenges they faced, the choices they made, and the values they upheld are woven into the fabric of our identity. By honoring their legacy, we acknowledge the profound impact they have had on our lives and the world around us.

The creative spark that ignited the dreams and aspirations of our ancestors continues to burn brightly within us. It is a testament to the enduring power of imagination and innovation, passed down through generations. This creative spirit drives us to explore new possibilities, push boundaries, and create a better future. In nurturing this spark, we honor the legacy of those who came before us and ensure that their contributions continue to inspire future generations.

THE LEGACY WE CARRY, STORIES OF FAMILY, COMMUNITY, AND THE CREATIVE SPARK THAT ENDURES

As we navigate the complexities of the modern world, the echoes of the past offer us a sense of grounding and perspective. They remind us of the values that have shaped our journey and the sacrifices that have paved the way for our progress. By listening to these echoes, we gain a deeper understanding of our heritage and the responsibility we carry in preserving and enhancing it. Our journey is a continuation of theirs, a testament to the enduring power of family, community, and the creative spark that binds us all.

5

Chapter 5: The Bonds That Bind

Family is the cornerstone of our existence, providing us with a sense of belonging and identity. The bonds that bind us to our loved ones are forged through shared experiences, mutual support, and unconditional love. These connections, though sometimes tested by the challenges of life, are a source of strength and resilience. They remind us of the importance of nurturing and cherishing the relationships that define us.

In the embrace of our families, we find comfort and solace. The warmth of a mother's hug, the wisdom in a father's words, and the laughter shared with siblings create a tapestry of memories that enrich our lives. These moments, though seemingly ordinary, are the building blocks of our identity. They shape our values, beliefs, and aspirations, guiding us as we navigate the complexities of the world.

The bonds of family extend beyond the immediate circle of parents and siblings. They encompass the broader network of relatives, friends, and community members who play a significant role in our lives. These connections, though varied in nature, are united by a common thread of love and support. They remind us of the importance of fostering a sense of community and belonging, and the impact it has on our well-being and growth.

As we move through life, the bonds that bind us to our loved ones serve as a source of inspiration and motivation. They remind us of the values that have been passed down through generations and the responsibility we carry in upholding them. In nurturing these relationships, we honor the legacy of our ancestors and ensure that the creative spark that defines us continues to burn brightly. Our journey is a testament to the enduring power of family, community, and the connections that shape us.

6

Chapter 6: Guardians of Wisdom

In every family, there are individuals who serve as the guardians of wisdom. These are the elders, whose lives are a testament to the resilience and strength that define our heritage. Their stories, experiences, and lessons are invaluable treasures that enrich our lives and guide our choices. As custodians of our collective memory, they play a crucial role in preserving the legacy we carry forward.

The wisdom of our elders is a beacon that illuminates the path ahead. Through their words and actions, they impart lessons of patience, perseverance, and compassion. Their experiences, shaped by the challenges and triumphs of their own journeys, offer us valuable insights into the complexities of life. By listening to their stories and heeding their advice, we gain a deeper understanding of the values that have sustained our families and communities through generations.

The relationship between elders and younger generations is a sacred bond, built on mutual respect and love. It is through this intergenerational connection that the wisdom of the past is transmitted and preserved. Grandparents become mentors, sharing their knowledge and experiences with their grandchildren. In turn, the younger generation brings fresh perspectives and ideas, ensuring that the legacy of wisdom continues to evolve and thrive.

As we navigate the ever-changing landscape of modern life, the wisdom of our elders offers us a sense of grounding and perspective. It reminds us of the importance of staying true to our values and honoring the legacy of those who came before us. By embracing the lessons of our elders, we ensure that their wisdom continues to inspire and guide us. Our journey is a testament to the enduring power of family, community, and the creative spark that binds us all.

7

Chapter 7: Celebrations of Life

Celebrations are a vibrant expression of the joy and vitality that define our existence. From birth to marriage to festivals, these moments of celebration are a testament to the richness and diversity of our cultural heritage. They offer us an opportunity to come together as a community, to honor our traditions, and to celebrate the milestones that mark our journey through life.

Each celebration is a tapestry of rituals, customs, and traditions that reflect the values and beliefs of our community. The rhythmic dances, the melodic songs, and the sumptuous feasts are all expressions of our collective spirit. These celebrations are not just events; they are experiences that strengthen the bonds of family and community. They remind us of the importance of unity, love, and gratitude in our lives.

In every culture, celebrations serve as a way to honor the past, celebrate the present, and inspire the future. They are a reflection of our shared experiences and a testament to the resilience and creativity that define us. Through these celebrations, we preserve the legacy of our ancestors and ensure that their traditions continue to thrive. They offer us a sense of continuity and connection, bridging the gap between generations.

As we continue to celebrate the milestones of our lives, we honor the legacy of those who came before us. Their traditions, customs, and values are woven into the fabric of our celebrations, enriching our experiences and inspiring our actions. By embracing these moments of joy and gratitude, we ensure that the creative spark that defines us continues to burn brightly. Our journey is a testament to the enduring power of family, community, and the celebrations that shape us.

8

Chapter 8: Journeys of Discovery

Life is a journey of discovery, filled with moments of exploration and self-realization. Each step we take, whether guided by curiosity or necessity, shapes our understanding of the world and our place within it. Our ancestors embarked on their own journeys, traversing unfamiliar landscapes and navigating uncharted waters. Their experiences of discovery and adaptation laid the groundwork for the lives we lead today, and their stories inspire us to embark on our own paths of exploration.

The journey of discovery is not limited to physical exploration; it extends to the realms of knowledge, creativity, and personal growth. Throughout history, individuals have pushed the boundaries of what is known, seeking answers to the mysteries of the universe and the intricacies of the human condition. Their quests for knowledge and understanding have enriched our collective wisdom, contributing to the legacy we inherit. In our own lives, the pursuit of learning and growth is a testament to the enduring creative spark that drives us.

Every discovery, no matter how small, is a step toward a greater understanding of ourselves and the world around us. These moments of realization and insight are the building blocks of our personal and collective journey. They remind us of the importance of curiosity, perseverance, and open-mindedness in our quest for knowledge and self-improvement. By embracing the spirit of discovery, we honor the legacy of those who came before us and ensure that their contributions continue to inspire future generations.

As we embark on our own journeys of discovery, we carry with us the lessons and experiences of our ancestors. Their stories of exploration and adaptation offer us valuable insights into the challenges and opportunities that lie ahead. By staying true to our values and nurturing our creative spark, we can navigate the complexities of the modern world and create our own legacies. Our journey is a testament to the enduring power of family, community, and the pursuit of knowledge and growth.

9

Chapter 9: The Power of Resilience

Resilience is the cornerstone of our journey through life, enabling us to withstand challenges and emerge stronger. Our ancestors faced countless obstacles and adversities, yet their unwavering determination and strength allowed them to persevere. Their stories of resilience serve as a source of inspiration and guidance, reminding us of the power we possess to overcome the difficulties we encounter.

In every family and community, there are countless examples of resilience. These stories, whether of personal triumph or collective struggle, reflect the indomitable spirit that defines our heritage. From the perseverance of a single mother raising her children to the solidarity of a community rebuilding after a disaster, these acts of resilience are a testament to the strength and courage that flow through our veins.

The creative spark within us is a powerful force that fuels our resilience. It is through creativity and innovation that we find solutions to challenges and opportunities for growth. Our ancestors harnessed their creative spirit to adapt to changing circumstances, and their legacy continues to inspire us. By embracing our creativity, we can navigate the uncertainties of life and build a future that reflects our values and aspirations.

As we face the trials and tribulations of modern life, the power of resilience offers us a sense of hope and possibility. It reminds us that we have the strength to overcome obstacles and the capacity to create positive change. By honoring the legacy of our resilient ancestors and nurturing our own creative spark, we can continue to thrive and inspire future generations. Our journey is a testament to the enduring power of family, community, and the resilience that defines us.

10

Chapter 10: Threads of Connection

In the intricate web of human experience, the threads of connection bind us together, creating a tapestry of relationships and shared moments. These connections, whether formed through family, friendship, or community, are the lifeblood of our existence. They offer us a sense of belonging and purpose, grounding us in the knowledge that we are part of something greater than ourselves.

The bonds we form with others are built on a foundation of trust, empathy, and mutual respect. They are nurtured through shared experiences, open communication, and acts of kindness. These connections enrich our lives, providing us with support and companionship as we navigate the ups and downs of our journey. In honoring these relationships, we acknowledge the importance of cultivating and maintaining the connections that define us.

The power of connection extends beyond the personal realm, influencing the broader fabric of our communities. When individuals come together with a shared sense of purpose and vision, they create a collective force that drives positive change. These communal bonds foster a sense of solidarity and unity, empowering us to address challenges and seize opportunities as a cohesive whole.

As we continue to build and strengthen our connections, we honor the legacy of those who came before us. Their stories of collaboration and mutual support serve as a guiding light, reminding us of the importance of unity and compassion. By nurturing the threads of connection, we ensure that the creative spark that binds us continues to thrive. Our journey is a testament to the enduring power of family, community, and the relationships that shape us.

11

Chapter 11: The Spirit of Generosity

Generosity is a hallmark of our shared humanity, reflecting the values of compassion, empathy, and selflessness. Throughout history, acts of kindness and generosity have played a pivotal role in shaping our communities and enhancing our collective well-being. These gestures, whether grand or modest, create a ripple effect that transcends time and space, leaving a lasting impact on the lives they touch.

In every family and community, there are stories of individuals who have gone above and beyond to support and uplift others. Their acts of generosity, whether through material resources, time, or emotional support, embody the spirit of altruism that defines our heritage. These stories serve as powerful reminders of the positive difference we can make in the lives of others when we act with an open heart and a giving spirit.

The creative spark within us is closely intertwined with the spirit of generosity. It is through sharing our talents, knowledge, and resources that we contribute to the growth and enrichment of our communities. Our ancestors understood the importance of giving back, and their legacy of generosity continues to inspire us. By embracing this spirit, we honor their contributions and ensure that the values of compassion and empathy endure.

As we navigate the complexities of the modern world, the spirit of generosity offers us a sense of hope and possibility. It reminds us that we have the power to create positive change, one act of kindness at a time. By cultivating a culture of generosity, we strengthen the bonds of family and community, ensuring that the creative spark that defines us continues to burn brightly. Our journey is a testament to the enduring power of family, community, and the spirit of giving that shapes us.

12

Chapter 12: The Journey of Change

Change is an inevitable part of life, shaping our experiences and guiding our evolution. Throughout history, individuals and communities have navigated periods of transformation, adapting to new circumstances and embracing new opportunities. These journeys of change, whether driven by necessity or choice, are a testament to the resilience and creativity that define our heritage.

The stories of our ancestors are filled with moments of change and adaptation. From migration to technological advancements, they embraced the challenges and opportunities that came their way. Their ability to navigate change with grace and ingenuity is a powerful reminder of the strength that lies within us. By honoring their legacy, we gain the courage to face our own journeys of change and growth.

The creative spark within us is a driving force that propels us forward in times of change. It is through creativity and innovation that we find solutions to the challenges we encounter and envision new possibilities for the future. Our ancestors harnessed their creative spirit to adapt to changing circumstances, and their legacy continues to inspire us. By nurturing this spark, we can navigate the complexities of the modern world and create a future that reflects our values and aspirations.

As we embark on our own journeys of change, we carry with us the lessons and experiences of those who came before us. Their stories of resilience and adaptation offer us valuable insights into the transformative power of change. By staying true to our values and embracing our creative spark, we can navigate the uncertainties of life and build a future that honors our heritage. Our journey is a testament to the enduring power of family, community, and the ability to embrace change.

13

Chapter 13: The Spirit of Innovation

Innovation is the lifeblood of progress, driving us to explore new possibilities and push the boundaries of what is known. Throughout history, individuals and communities have harnessed their creative spirit to develop new technologies, ideas, and solutions. These innovations have shaped our world, transforming the way we live, work, and connect with one another.

The stories of our ancestors are filled with examples of innovation and ingenuity. From the development of new agricultural techniques to the creation of intricate artworks, their contributions have left a lasting impact on our heritage. These acts of innovation are a testament to the power of human creativity and the desire to improve our lives and the world around us. By honoring their legacy, we are inspired to continue exploring new possibilities and pushing the boundaries of what is possible.

The creative spark within us is a powerful force that fuels our drive for innovation. It is through creativity and imagination that we envision new solutions to the challenges we face and create a future that reflects our values and aspirations. Our ancestors understood the importance of nurturing this spark, and their legacy continues to inspire us. By embracing our creative spirit, we can navigate the complexities of the modern world and contribute to the ongoing legacy of innovation.

As we embark on our own journeys of innovation, we carry with us the lessons and experiences of those who came before us. Their stories of creativity and ingenuity offer us valuable insights into the transformative power of innovation. By staying true to our values and nurturing our creative spark, we can continue to explore new possibilities and create a future that honors our heritage. Our journey is a testament to the enduring power of family, community, and the spirit of innovation.

14

Chapter 14: The Strength of Unity

Unity is a powerful force that binds us together, creating a sense of solidarity and collective strength. Throughout history, individuals and communities have come together to overcome challenges, support one another, and create positive change. These acts of unity are a testament to the enduring power of collaboration and mutual support.

The stories of our ancestors are filled with examples of unity and cooperation. From the efforts of communities to rebuild after a disaster to the solidarity of social movements, their collective actions have left a lasting impact on our heritage. These acts of unity remind us of the importance of working together and supporting one another in times of need. By honoring their legacy, we are inspired to continue fostering a sense of unity and solidarity in our own lives.

The creative spark within us is closely intertwined with the spirit of unity. It is through collaboration and mutual support that we can achieve great things and create a better future. Our ancestors understood the importance of working together, and their legacy continues to inspire us. By embracing the spirit of unity, we can navigate the complexities of the modern world and create positive change in our communities.

As we continue to build and strengthen our connections, we honor the legacy of those who came before us. Their stories of collaboration and mutual support serve as a guiding light, reminding us of the importance of unity and compassion. By nurturing the threads of connection, we ensure that the creative spark that binds us continues to thrive. Our journey is a testament to the enduring power of family, community, and the strength of unity.

15

Chapter 15: The Role of Mentorship

Mentorship is a powerful force that shapes our personal and professional growth. Throughout history, individuals have sought guidance and support from mentors who offer wisdom, experience, and encouragement. These relationships are a testament to the enduring power of knowledge sharing and the impact of one generation's experiences on the next.

The stories of our ancestors are filled with examples of mentorship and guidance. From the apprenticeships of craftsmen to the teachings of scholars, mentorship has played a crucial role in passing down skills, knowledge, and values. These relationships are a reflection of the creative spark that drives us to learn and grow. By honoring the legacy of our mentors, we ensure that their contributions continue to inspire future generations.

The relationship between mentor and mentee is built on a foundation of trust, respect, and mutual growth. It is through this connection that valuable lessons and insights are transmitted, enriching both the mentor and the mentee. The guidance of a mentor offers us a sense of direction and purpose, helping us navigate the complexities of life and achieve our aspirations.

As we continue to seek and offer mentorship, we honor the legacy of those who came before us. Their stories of guidance and support serve as a beacon, reminding us of the importance of nurturing the next generation. By embracing the spirit of mentorship, we ensure that the creative spark that defines us continues to thrive. Our journey is a testament to the enduring power of family, community, and the role of mentorship in shaping our lives.

16

Chapter 16: The Journey of Healing

Healing is an integral part of our journey, allowing us to process pain, overcome challenges, and find peace. Throughout history, individuals and communities have sought ways to heal from physical, emotional, and spiritual wounds. The stories of healing are a testament to the resilience and strength that define our heritage.

The stories of our ancestors are filled with moments of healing and recovery. From traditional remedies and rituals to acts of forgiveness and reconciliation, their experiences offer valuable lessons in the power of healing. These stories remind us of the importance of addressing our wounds and finding ways to move forward with grace and resilience.

The creative spark within us plays a crucial role in the healing process. It is through artistic expression, storytelling, and connection that we find ways to process our pain and transform it into something meaningful. Our ancestors harnessed their creative spirit to heal from their own challenges, and their legacy continues to inspire us. By embracing our creativity, we can navigate the healing journey and find strength in our experiences.

As we embark on our own journeys of healing, we carry with us the lessons and experiences of those who came before us. Their stories of resilience and recovery offer us valuable insights into the transformative power of healing. By staying true to our values and nurturing our creative spark, we can navigate the complexities of the modern world and create a future that honors our heritage. Our journey is a testament to the enduring power of family, community, and the journey of healing.

17

Chapter 17: A Legacy of Hope

Hope is the light that guides us through the darkest times, offering us a sense of possibility and promise. Throughout history, individuals and communities have held onto hope as a source of strength and inspiration. The stories of hope are a testament to the enduring spirit that defines our heritage and the creative spark that drives us forward.

The stories of our ancestors are filled with moments of hope and aspiration. From the dreams of a better future to the determination to overcome adversity, their experiences are a reflection of the power of hope. These stories remind us of the importance of staying true to our values and holding onto our dreams, even in the face of challenges.

The creative spark within us is a powerful force that fuels our sense of hope. It is through creativity and imagination that we envision new possibilities and create a future that reflects our values and aspirations. Our ancestors understood the importance of nurturing this spark, and their legacy continues to inspire us. By embracing our creative spirit, we can navigate the complexities of the modern world and contribute to the ongoing legacy of hope.

As we continue to carry the legacy of hope, we honor the stories and experiences of those who came before us. Their determination and resilience offer us valuable insights into the transformative power of hope. By staying true to our values and nurturing our creative spark, we can create a future that honors our heritage and inspires future generations. Our journey is a testament to the enduring power of family, community, and the legacy of hope.

18

Chapter 18: The Essence of Identity

Identity is the essence of our being, shaped by the stories, values, and experiences that define us. Throughout history, individuals and communities have navigated the complexities of identity, seeking to understand themselves and their place in the world. The stories of our ancestors offer valuable insights into the multifaceted nature of identity and the ways in which it evolves over time.

The journey of self-discovery is a lifelong process, influenced by our heritage, culture, and personal experiences. Our ancestors embarked on their own journeys of identity, grappling with questions of belonging and purpose. Their stories, filled with moments of introspection and revelation, serve as a guide for our own exploration of identity. By honoring their legacy, we gain a deeper understanding of ourselves and the values that define us.

The creative spark within us plays a crucial role in the formation of identity. It is through artistic expression, storytelling, and connection that we explore and articulate our sense of self. Our ancestors understood the importance of creativity in the journey of identity, and their legacy continues to inspire us. By embracing our creative spirit, we can navigate the complexities of identity and create a future that reflects our values and aspirations.

As we continue to explore and define our identity, we carry with us the lessons and experiences of those who came before us. Their stories of self-discovery and growth offer us valuable insights into the transformative power of identity. By staying true to our values and nurturing our creative spark, we can navigate the complexities of the modern world and create a future that honors our heritage. Our journey is a testament to the enduring power of family, community, and the essence of identity.

19

Chapter 19: A Legacy of Love

Love is the foundation of our existence, nurturing our hearts and souls and guiding our actions. Throughout history, individuals and communities have experienced the transformative power of love, building connections and creating bonds that transcend time and space. The stories of love are a testament to the enduring spirit that defines our heritage and the creative spark that drives us forward.

The stories of our ancestors are filled with moments of love and connection. From the tender embrace of a parent to the unwavering support of a partner, their experiences are a reflection of the power of love. These stories remind us of the importance of nurturing our relationships and cherishing the moments of connection that enrich our lives.

The creative spark within us is closely intertwined with the power of love. It is through creativity and imagination that we express our love and create a future that reflects our values and aspirations. Our ancestors understood the importance of nurturing this spark, and their legacy continues to inspire us. By embracing our creative spirit, we can navigate the complexities of the modern world and contribute to the ongoing legacy of love.

As we continue to carry the legacy of love, we honor the stories and experiences of those who came before us. Their determination and resilience offer us valuable insights into the transformative power of love. By staying true to our values and nurturing our creative spark, we can create a future that honors our heritage and inspires future generations. Our journey is a testament to the enduring power of family, community, and the legacy of love.

Book Description:

In "The Legacy We Carry," we embark on a heartfelt journey through the rich tapestry of family, community, and creativity that shapes our lives. This evocative collection of stories celebrates the resilience, love, and ingenuity of our ancestors, weaving together their triumphs and struggles to create a vivid portrait of our shared heritage.

From the roots of our journey, where tradition and wisdom are passed down through generations, to the vibrant celebrations that unite us, each chapter delves into the essence of what it means to be part of a family and community. The tales of innovation, resilience, and hope highlight the creative spark that drives us forward, while the enduring bonds of love and connection remind us of the strength we draw from one another.

Through the lens of personal and collective experiences, "The Legacy We Carry" offers a profound exploration of identity, healing, and the transformative power of mentorship. As we honor the legacy of those who came before us, we are inspired to embrace our own journeys of discovery and growth, nurturing the creative spirit that defines us.

Join us in this celebration of the enduring power of family, community, and the creative spark that binds us all. "The Legacy We Carry" is a testament to the strength, unity, and love that shape our lives and illuminate our paths.

www.ingramcontent.com/pod-product-compliance
Lightning Source LLC
LaVergne TN
LVHW020456080526
838202LV00057B/5984